TRACKS ACROSS THE BEACH

Peter Smith

Illustrated by Graham Clarke

Scripture Union is an international Christian charity working with churches in more than 130 countries, providing resources to bring the good news about Jesus to children, young people and families and to encourage them to develop spiritually through the Bible and prayer.

Scripture Union, 207–209 Queensway, Bletchley, Milton Keynes,
MK2 2EB, England
Email: info@scriptureunion.org.uk
Website: www.scriptureunion.org.uk

British Library Cataloguing-in-Publication Data.
A catalogue record of this book is available from the British Library
Illustrations by Graham Clarke
Cover and page design by David Lund
Printed and bound in Singapore by Tien Wah Press (Pte) Ltd.

Foreword

'Her ways are ways of pleasantness, and all her paths are peace'
(Proverbs 3:17).

Here is a description of wisdom, and this book you will find is a wise
book. In it we are invited to share the walk of faith with an
experienced guide, who gently but firmly takes us along known
paths, and helps us realise what we may have missed by their very
familiarity. He takes us also into new territory, and gives us the
confidence we need to press on, undeterred by its demands. What
glorious scenery is presented to us on the way, through the breath-
takingly beautiful watercolours, feasts for our eyes and hearts.
Geography and theology combine to draw us into a closer and deeper
relationship with God.

In the busy, demanding and often confusing world we find ourselves
part of today, it is sometimes difficult to find our way. Within these
pages and pictures we can slow down, rediscover the ways of pleasantness and the paths of peace, and know the presence and power of Jesus,
the one who is 'the way, the truth and the life'. I commend the book
and the journey to you – look out for the signposts, heed the directions,
and enjoy each step.

Margaret Cundiff
(Author and broadcaster)

To Iris May Bird (Helen's Mum)
Her laughter and enthusiasm
for life
and true love for others
have been an inspiration to me

Contents

1 · DECISIONS

5 · COMMUNICATING BY PRAYER

9 · BE QUIET

13 · SLOW DOWN

17 · THE NEED FOR A PLAN

21 · A NEW START

25 · START WALKING IN FAITH

29 · STARTING AGAIN

33 · TURNING POINTS

37 · A WALK TO THE CROSS

41 · A WALK WITH THE CROSS

45 · A CONTENTED WALK

49 · CELEBRATION ALONG THE WAY

53 · FREEDOM TO WALK OUR OWN WAY

Acknowledgements

I would like to thank Graham, not only for his willingness to let me include some of his wonderful watercolours, but also for his enthusiasm and support. His professionalism, energy and good humour have been a great encouragement, especially for one with no experience in this kind of project. I would also like to thank Andrew and the team at Scripture Union for making my ideas for this book a reality.

Thank you, Margaret, for your foreword, and for your advice and encouragement as I set about transferring thoughts and ideas to paper. Your writings and your example of faith have personally helped me in making my own way and I thank you for your part in this venture.

Many people have encouraged me to put my experiences and thoughts down in print. I deeply appreciate the support of family and friends at church and at school. I would like to thank Margaret for reading the text and helping me with the questions at the end of each chapter. Especially I want to thank Christine who, throughout the project, has supported me with her prayers and words of encouragement. Thanks to Diane, too, for reading the script and offering her feelings and reactions in an honest and loving way. Both Christine and Diane have done much more than they realise in making this book a reality. Neither will ever admit to this.

Thank you to my wife, Helen, for her constant love, support and prayers. Without her tolerance and patience and the good humour, and the loving support of my daughters Sarah and Ali, there is no way that I would have completed this book.

Introduction

It may sound grand, but by setting out in faith we all begin a personal walk of discovery. None of us walk the same route or the same way. We all see things differently along our walk, viewing landscapes and experiencing situations from our own perspective. We mount our stiles, cross bridges, turn new corners and see our rainbows at different times, in different places. Our walk is shaped by the people we meet, the situations we face and the experiences we share.

My experiences, as a teacher in a secondary school for twenty-two years, more recently as a deputy headteacher and as a reader in my local parish church, together with being husband and dad, have influenced my faith. A few of these I refer to in this book. Many events and people have directed and redirected my walk and I mention some of them, although the names are made up. Yet I still find myself, at home or at school or anywhere else, thinking: 'Lord, which way now?' 'Is this the right way?' 'Lord, why this way?'

In one of those precious, all too rare, quiet moments, close your eyes and try to imagine a golden sandy beach, your beach, stretching towards the horizon. Why a beach? Perhaps it is all those happy memories of geography fieldcourses spent transecting sand dunes! Or perhaps it is because I look forward to summer holidays so much. On your beach you see many tracks in the sand, taking off in different directions, some ending up at the water's edge, others disappearing into the dunes. Which track do you follow? To complicate things, sandy beaches normally change. Tracks disappear as the tide comes in, new ones appear. Dunes change shape with the wind, new pathways emerge. So too with our walk of faith. Which track, how long? I have no hesitation in saying that a right decision is difficult. However, I am sure that they are God's tracks and he will help us decide.

You may ask: 'If every journey is personal, why these reflections?' They are only my signposts, real life reflections based upon my experience. I hope they will be of value to you, too, in helping you reflect on your walk of faith.

The watercolours included with these reflections were painted by Graham Clarke, a friend who is an internationally-known local artist. Graham's water-colours are my personal choice, selected from a large number of originals. Each one speaks to me and helps me put my thoughts into perspective. I hope they speak to you too.

Chapter One

Nothing can prepare you for your first day, week or even year of teaching – not university, not life's experiences, not even teaching practice. Anticipating your first classes' arrival after all your anxious preparation is very daunting. How will they get on making the model of a volcano? Will Richard behave himself with the PVA glue? And what mood will Tom be in this Friday afternoon, last period? Pacing the floor during my first year, dreading that last period on a Friday with Year 10, is a nightmare I still, on occasions, relive.

The lesson rarely went according to plan. Richard often messed around and so ended up in Monday's detention. He broke a light bulb once, when he threw something across the room harder than he meant too. It was the afternoon I had promised to arrange some fieldwork on the school playing fields, but it poured with rain. Richard always wanted to be the centre of attention. That same afternoon, he tried opening the classroom door and the inside handle came off. Imagine being trapped with a large group of hyperactive 16 year olds, disappointed because it was raining and they weren't going outside. Richard was there, proudly displaying the door handle as a newly-found toy. Believe me, such situations call for quick decisions. The first year in teaching, it seems, is full of making decisions, decisions based upon very little experience!

Like parents, teachers are constantly asked: where? which? when? what? and why? Decisions, decisions! As children grow up they take on the responsibility of making decisions, from choices about school dinners to GCSE subjects, from the choice of which coloured pen to use to which career to aim at, decisions about right and wrong, about what is important and of real value. Teachers, like parents and other adults, influence this process, and although this is a privilege it is also a frightening challenge.

We all know that some decisions have to be made immediately, while others need careful consideration. And the working party and committee are not always the best methods of effective decision-making. Ask any teacher or member of a Church Council! As Deputy Head I have sat through endless discussions that end with no decision being made. Life is all about decisions, some of which, as we all know, are hard and painful. This applies to our Christian walk too.

Our first watercolour, of Dungeness, Kent, depicts a scene which could hardly be more different from our imaginary beach. Gone are the golden sandy dunes and palm trees to be replaced by coarse pebbles with an occasional seakale plant. The relaxed atmosphere on a sun-drenched beach is replaced by a traditional and workmanlike scene. Tracks lead off in different directions. Our eyes follow just one track, used for transporting fish boxes across the shingle to the boats. One track, one purpose…

The Bible has illustrations of many people making a personal decision. In the Book of Genesis, Abraham receives God's message to leave his native land and familiar surroundings and go to a new land. God gives no reason as to why Abraham is chosen. There is no evidence as to what his feelings were. What preparation had he done? What skills or experience did he have? How did he really feel? As well as being

surprised, was he also pleased and excited or angry and depressed? Did he feel inadequate? Was he stressed out? Jacob, Joseph, Isaiah, Job, Jonah, Elijah and Samuel all had unfamiliar tracks to follow too. How did Moses react when told of his mission to lead his people from captivity in Egypt? We know that Samuel wasn't expecting that God would speak to him and his call, in the middle of the night, was a great surprise. And as for the wise men, how unsure were they as tracks opened up for them across the desert towards Bethlehem, illuminated by a star?

Were these people special? Only in the sense that they were chosen by God. Was the path, for them, as clear as the track on Dungeness beach? Did they know why they had to follow such a track? Simon and Andrew, two fishermen brothers from Bethsaida, were literally sitting on the beach at Capernaum when a new track opened up for them as they met Jesus and heard his call. Something similar occurred to all the disciples.

The future path was far from clear for them.

However, these people seemed to be decisive. Even with all the uncertainty they pressed on. As the Bible shows, they all made mistakes. They all were sometimes depressed as well as elated, disillusioned and frightened as well as full of hope in the confidence of God's message. In all cases it was a real roller-coaster journey. Yet in it all God's guidance was there when needed, and his presence very real.

In school it is often a proud moment when we welcome former pupils back for a visit. Richard came in a few months ago. He is 35 years old now, happily married with a little boy. He runs his own business selling all kinds of doors (I hope they have safe handles!). He is a practising Christian and runs a local youth group, regularly organising Christian events in Kent. He is so much more confident and happier than in his younger days when family problems resulted in a truly unstable and insecure life.

Simon Peter, after the Resurrection, met a man on the beach of Lake Galilee. He had been fishing and caught nothing until the man told Peter to fish on the other side of the boat. He caught loads of fish, and on the beach they ate and talked. Then Jesus set out Peter's tracks: 'Feed my sheep, build my church'. Knowing that Jesus still had work for him to do must have been a great boost for Peter.

Finding God on our beach is often difficult. Speaking and listening to him to find out which track to follow may be a great challenge. But you never know. Perhaps like Peter our own tracks may lead, as they do in this watercolour, to a new fishing business, God's business.

'The LORD had said to Abram, "Leave your country, your people and your father's household and go to the land I will show you"...So Abram left as the LORD had told him; and Lot went with him.' (Genesis 12:1,4). Do you believe that God can map out a clear path for us? How can we know which track to follow? Have you recognised any recently?

Have you ever experienced God's call to do something unexpected? How did you respond?

Chapter Two

I am not particularly keen on roller coaster rides. I have braved some with my children and while on outings from school, but the ones I choose are not the adventurous, loop-the-loop or 'sheer-drop' type. I just succumb to the cries, 'Come on sir, it's only a mild one!' And the attendant always says, 'Hold on tight and enjoy the ride'. All I can think of is the sheer terror of what is in store and I ask myself, 'Why am I doing this and why is this person encouraging me to enjoy myself?' Then I think, 'I could pray about it!' There I am, surrounded by people screaming with enjoyment, anticipation and excitement, laughing and waving their hands in the air, wanting to pray about a safe return to the start as quickly as possible. As members of my family or large numbers of Year 7 pupils witness my every move, keen to highlight my embarrassment and lack of comfort, I can only pray that I *do* return, if somewhat worse for wear after an agonising ordeal – all in the name of 'fun'!

What a situation for prayer! I have always been a little confused about where and how to pray and what to pray about, yet I know that to be in touch with God I need to pray. For any of us to decide on a track to follow, we need to be in touch with God. Sometimes, though, through frustration, indecision or even through anger I find it difficult to pray. Sometimes because I am enjoying or busying myself so much, I forget. And when I do find a way and a time, then will God listen? How will I know what he says? On that roller-coaster going down every dip (steep dip for me!), every jerk from side to side, every plunge into darkness, there I am praying: 'Lord I hope you are there!'

Along my tracks, I often sense myself praying exactly that. At school there are many times when I feel the need to pray. As Head of Sixth Form I talk with many older teenage students about their studies, their concerns and worries, and about their aspirations. It is a real privilege to listen to their deep anxieties as well as their wildest dreams and exciting experiences. I try to listen and not to talk too much. Take Simon, for instance. I called him into my office to discuss the lack of progress in his studies, his lack of concentration and motivation, and his absence from school. We talked about how his father had walked out on his family a few years ago and about how his mother's boyfriend had become violent, hitting his younger sister and threatening his mother. Simon had become the stabilising influence, the person his mother and sister relied upon, and that is why his work had suffered. He cried as he told me that his sister wanted to leave home and described his attempts to get the boyfriend to leave. He told me the boyfriend had now gone, but for how long?

Part of me wanted to discipline him for his attitude to work, but another part urged me to pray with him, asking for guidance both for Simon and myself. If only other people, quick to judge and condemn, knew Simon's real situation.

There is also the case of Andrew. Only a week or so ago, he came to see me and immediately started crying, asking me to listen. He had passed his driving test on Monday. On Tuesday, driving his car for the first time, he had hit a concrete post while parking. His parents, who, as

he had told me previously, were on the verge of splitting up, were upset, blaming each other, but were also sympathetic, warning him about the need to take more care. On Friday he had hit a van on the way to school, mistaking the van driver's intention to turn right. He sobbed as he said that he couldn't confess to his parents yet again.

I advised him, but I am not a counsellor, merely a teacher. I prayed about him and his parents, and about what I had said. All this came before an important meeting with the rest of the Senior Management Team about the school budget. It was also the day when the school shut early because of a major flood warning in the centre of Maidstone. No buses would be running after 1.30pm. As well as having Andrew's worries on my mind, I was praying that we would get home safely.

Prayer is vital. Frequently I find I want to shoot arrow prayers to God. It is a kind of 'responsible thinking'. Events happen, situations arise, decisions have to be made and we need this two-way communication. It is often very difficult to pray but prayer is the only way of offering our problems, failures, anxieties, experiences and successes to God and trying to identify God's thoughts and feelings in return.

I often think what it must have been like to be one of Jesus' disciples. Peter and Andrew were fishermen by trade. Scenes like that at Dungeness, in our next watercolour, would have been familiar to them. Activities associated with fishing, reflected in the picture, were part of everyday life for them, sometimes bringing success, at other times despair and failure. Their life focussed around the repairing of boats, mending nets, watching the weather, finding the best location on the lake to fish.

It is not surprising, therefore, that Peter, Andrew, and the other disciples found it difficult to pray. They had no special training. Remember how they fell asleep when Jesus asked them to keep awake and pray with him? Many times when Jesus prayed to his Father they wondered what he was doing and why. Yet Jesus always emphasised the need to pray. He told us not to pray by using meaningless words and shouting them at the street corner. He directed our prayer through his own, by giving us the words of the Lord's Prayer, encouraging us to pray to our Father in heaven that his will be done on earth as it is in heaven.

My ride on the 'mild' roller coaster was an experience. I survived. I am not sure how I looked as the attendant said afterwards, 'It wasn't that bad, was it?' No it wasn't. We had travelled up slope, down, dipped, been yanked about and hurled from side to side and then we had gone back to the start and gone round again! Tracks on our beach may not be easy to follow at times. They may take us back to the beginning to start again. The track on Dungeness Beach leads to the boat, and the purpose of it all – fishing. We need to pray about our purpose too.

How often do you wonder if God is there and listening to you? At such times, do you dare pray like this: 'Why, O LORD do you stand far off? Why do you hide yourself in times of trouble?' (Psalm 10:1)

Fairfield Church

Chapter three

The church in the watercolour is Fairfield Church, one of the Romney Marsh churches, not far from Dungeness. The watercolour seems to capture the unique beauty of a Marshland scene. The landscape exudes a stillness characteristic of this part of the south of England. Our eyes, focusing on this small, historic church, located in green pasture, cannot help but absorb an inner peace and tranquillity that is God's own.

In our busyness we often find it difficult to experience peace. It seems almost impossible to find a quiet time and place to communicate with God. At school, as all teachers will agree, we lurch from one crisis to another during our working day, finding little opportunity to think about our teaching, and even less time to pray about it. Yet as Christians we believe that everywhere we go and whatever we do God is trying to attract our attention and to convey a message. Too often we are not expecting him to do this because the context is so ordinary. Because we only look for God in out-of-the-ordinary events and circumstances, we miss him in the everyday.

In the Old Testament a picture is painted of a figure standing on a cliff ledge, outside a cave, struggling against the natural elements of earthquake, wind and thunderstorm. The natural violence must have seemed too intense for anyone to bear, but Elijah somehow managed to survive. Standing on Mount Horeb, in the middle of the storm, Elijah believed his life's work to be in ruins. Yet back inside, in the stillness of the cave, he hears a quiet, almost inaudible voice. In the quietness, God speaks to his servant. Elijah was doubtless looking to God to communicate and act through the storm, but he heard nothing. It was only in the quiet place that God's faint voice was heard. This voice gave Elijah renewed hope and confidence and set out his future tracks for him.

This Bible picture reveals a lot about God's character which is important for us. Elijah learnt, in a terrifying fashion, that God is not always in the spectacular, and that even in the midst of the most dramatic and stormy circumstances God may well speak in a quiet way.

Fairfield Church

I think of this picture when I visit dramatic locations in stormy weather. I remember experiencing feelings of excitement, mixed with sheer fright, when I was in the Glenderlough Valley in Ireland during a violent storm one afternoon. The round stone towers and Celtic crosses, set against a backdrop of dark thunderous skies, flashes of lightning and claps of thunder made for a disturbing atmosphere. I remember thinking of the religious significance of this scene. Perhaps God was speaking in this context? In the early evening the atmosphere was still and the storm had passed. Was God more likely to be speaking then?

God is often found in mundane, commonplace events, and we therefore often look in the wrong place for him. Thinking of this, I am reminded of a fieldwork venture, to Sheerness on the Isle of Sheppey. After a successful morning spent assessing coastal management strategies and recording shop types, leisure facilities, pedestrian numbers, and the views of residents, I realised I had lost my car keys. The whole party was bludgeoned into retracing steps in a vain attempt to find them. Fortunately we had some time in hand before we were due to study cliff formation at Warren Point. Everyone helped, some very enthusiastically, combing the promenade thoroughly, while others begrudgingly walked along the High Street yet again.

We gave up and continued the fieldwork. Returning home, I rang the police station in Sheerness. They had my keys, identified by a distinctive keyring. A kind person had handed them in immediately after I had lost them, in the centre of town. I hadn't thought to enquire. All the time we were looking in the wrong place when the logical place to ask was at the police station.

Finding God is a little like this frantic search. Sometimes we may want to look enthusiastically for God, whereas on other occasions our efforts are less serious or diligent. We may give up at times. Many people do not search or even want to look at all, seeing it as an irrelevant waste of time and effort. Yet God is there, in the ordinary people and events that affect us.

The Bible records many occasions when God's presence was experienced by ordinary people in ordinary situations. Joseph found God in a dream, Samuel heard God while sleeping in the tabernacle, shepherds learned about the birth of Jesus while tending their sheep on the hillslopes above Bethlehem, and fishermen mending their nets at the lakeside were called to be disciples. Jesus was in a garden when he was betrayed, and after his Resurrection he appeared to his disciples on a beach. God was found to be communicating in the context of ordinary life. Sometimes he spoke in dramatic ways, but often he spoke in the stillness, in a voice that was sometimes barely audible.

It is difficult, for me, to find quiet moments when I am able to listen. The hectic hustle and bustle, at school and home, makes only the briefest of arrow prayers possible and finding out their effectiveness is often impossible. Yet too much busyness and impatience makes us forget the quiet patience we need. Dietrich Bonhoeffer writes in his book *Life Together*: 'Silence is the simple stillness of the individual under the word of God….We are silent at the beginning of the day because God should have the first word and we are silent before going to sleep because the last word also belongs to God.' When these moments occur they allow us to listen and reflect rather than just request and look for guidance.

'Be still, and know that I am God' (Psalm 46:10). Do you find it so difficult to make time to be still for quiet reflection and prayer?

What experience have you had recently of God speaking to you in the ordinary circumstances of life? (Were you surprised?)

Chapter Four

When I watch football matches on the TV these days the small digital clock, relentlessly ticking on through the match in the top left hand corner of the screen, concerns me. If the team we want to win is leading, the time cannot go quick enough; we are desperate for the clock to go faster. If our team is losing we want the clock to slow down or even to stop. But we cannot do anything about the passing of time. The digital clock ticks on as the match goes on: kick off, half time, full time, injury time, extra time, penalty shoot out time. Won or lost, another match is over.

As the digital clock ticks on, so too do our lives. One day soon I will be 393,120 hours old (the equivalent of 262,080 football matches). Of these hours I will have spent approximately 35,880 of them teaching and it feels like it too! I have spent approximately 114,660 hours asleep (the equivalent of 13 years). What a thought! Analysis like this, while keeping school statisticians happy, is as frightening as it is fascinating. How we spend time – eating, travelling, shopping, working, sitting in committee meetings, pursuing hobbies, watching TV, sleeping – is interesting but also scary.

This is why I like the watercolour of the old man outside his cottage. It is a quaint, traditional scene at Dungeness; the fisherman's cottage is typical of those found along the shingle beach in this area. They seem ramshackle yet they resist the worst kind of weather in this exposed location. The old man reads, with the world passing him by as though he is in a time warp. I long for times like this, on holidays for example, when time seems of no consequence, with no pressures, no rush, no deadlines.

It is interesting, too, to think of the occasions when unexpected events provide time, when circumstances almost force time to stand still. On a return school journey across the Irish Sea, I remember the weather being stormy when we arrived at Dun Laoghaire. Our sailing was delayed for most of the day. We departed late at night, and the weather had put Holyhead's harbour lights out of action. Our long journey was extended for another four hours before enough light and calmer seas allowed us to dock. For the whole day and night, time seemed to stand still. Extra and enforced time spent with a party of school pupils feeling somewhat seasick and anxious to get home was not a thrilling experience. Should these times, though, be full of stress and panic as uncertainty sets in, or can they be used for quiet reflection, for listening, for letting the world go by as we resign ourselves to an enforced time of inactivity?

This reminds me of the storm on Lake Galilee. The disciples crewed the boat while Jesus was asleep. When an unexpected storm occured, the disciples panicked and reacted by frantically waking Jesus, who rather than ignoring or condemning their panic, eased their fears by calming the storm. He saw this as an opportunity to show the disciples that God cares, that he can be trusted and, however unexpected the circumstances, God responds positively. He has power over everything, even time.

So whether it was at times set deliberately aside or in those unexpected circumstances Jesus lived for every present moment and was not pleased when people were always anxious about the future. In Matthew's Gospel Jesus is quoted as saying: 'Who of you by worrying can add a single hour to his life?.... Do not worry about tomorrow, for tomorrow will worry about itself.' (Matthew 6:27, 34). And Jesus practised what he preached. Even as the hour of the Cross was approaching Jesus treasured every difficult moment, using time as a friend not an enemy – an opportunity for loving, helping, sharing.

I find this difficult, as a teacher's working day, probably more than that of most other professionals, is structured by the clock. No sooner is registration over than it is assembly time, lesson time, break time, then lesson, lunch, lesson, meetings. As the bell sounds, so our lives change direction. We see new faces, teach new or different things, meet new challenges and face new opportunities. Until the bell sounds again!

I am sure that we all try to fight against the clock, moaning that we never have time. Yet Jesus says that we should use every moment, however mundane and routine the task. Mother Teresa once wrote: 'Today we have no time, even to look at each other, to talk to each other, to enjoy each other. And so less and less are we in touch with each other. The world is lost for want of sweetness and kindness. People are starving for love because everyone is in such a great rush.'

Sound bites seem to be so important today. Our politics, education, even our churches operate by sound bites. Our beautiful world, even our family and friends are seen in sound bites. Somehow, though, our walk must be more than this. Jesus always seemed to have time to be an important part of so many people's lives. He had time to explain his teaching, to talk to children, to heal, to socialise with friends and undesirables alike, time to pray quietly and be alone.

At the unexpected times, when I am forced to be inactive and slow down, I think of people unable to do much because of their fear, disability, loneliness, poverty or hunger. Yet so many of these people still manage to achieve many positive things with their time. I keep looking at the old man as he sits and reads outside his cottage and thinking how Christmas, Easter and summer holidays speed by. My prayer is, 'Slow me down, Lord. Make me reflect on the best use of my beach tracks today'. I believe that Jesus' Resurrection is about the future, but it is also a present reality as well. 'Jesus, walk with me today'.

Paul encourages us to 'make the most of every opportunity' (Colossians 4:5). How can we best use our time and opportunities to tell other people what God is doing for us and what he can do for them?

The Psalmist writes, 'My times are in your hands' (Psalm 31:15). In Isaiah we read, 'Blessed are all who wait for him (the LORD)!' How can we apply these truths to our everyday lives?

Chapter Five

Finding time to be quiet is difficult enough but planning activities through the day is even more of a problem. I always see planning as important because it makes the most effective use of time. But there are many days that do not go to plan at all. It seems strange, in my work at school, that every aspect, such as the curriculum, capital expenditure, budget and roll forecasts, is directed towards long-term strategic planning but hardly a day goes by when my plans do not change, sometimes completely. The more I am forced to live by my diary, planning months if not years in advance, the more my daily commitments seem to take me by surprise. This is true at home but it is especially true at school.

I remember one January afternoon when a man dressed as an official workman came into the School Office, saying that he had been sent by the Local Authority. He offered to use leftover tarmac from motorway maintenance work for resurfacing the playground areas. The Headmaster and I discussed the situation, agreeing that this would be a good idea. I was left to complete the details. Next morning the man returned complete with machinery and a band of workman. They did the work very quickly and he presented me with the bill. The amount was so inflated that, for such a short working time, it was unbelievable. He argued that I had signed to confirm £x per sqare metre. I realised I had been conned. By now it was break-time with hundreds of students streaming out of school and taking up vantage points to watch my every move.

I tried to keep calm, refusing to pay, asking him to step inside to discuss the matter. He refused and began shouting accusations at me for breaking our contract. I realised I did not have permission to pay this money and I argued my case. His ranting and raving continued, fully audible to our audience and I was called many names, most of them unprintable. I tried an arrow prayer for help as I had hundreds of pairs of eyes focussed on my reactions, on my decisions.

By now I had been joined by the Headmaster and a policeman who was visiting the school to take part in a Year 10 social education lesson. The irate man was escorted from the premises shouting abuse, demanding full payment, and threatening to sue the school. I was commended in the afternoon Assembly for my calmness and patience in a difficult situation, but I didn't feel like celebrating.

My pride had been dented; I felt a failure and I felt frightened of the consequences, even of driving home. I had been conned and the school was to suffer financially by having to pay the large if reduced bill. At the solicitor's office, I had to hand over payment to the man in question. It was an embarrassing and humbling experience and one of which some staff still remind me. That series of events completely upset my plans for many days, if not weeks, afterwards.

On reflection, I learnt much in that tricky situation and I felt God's hand in it. I prayed about the incident afterwards and I felt that he revealed positive directions forward, in an encouraging and constructive way. My calmness and patience did come through, and were identified and praised. My need to be more careful in certain contexts proved to be a lesson from which I still learn today.

Was God intervening in my life, wanting me to be involved in something totally unplanned? For all of us, our day may be mapped out, our diary organised and our time filled when a telephone call occurs, an unexpected visitor arrives, an unscheduled meeting or event happens which upsets all our plans. Sometimes this disturbances of our routine may cause disappointment, resentment, even anger. But we must be prepared for this as we make tracks. Possibly, though, such interruptions may lead to a joyous or exciting experience, a new partnership or relationship. Changes to plans, then, can lead to something special and wonderful.

It made me think. My life is so conditioned to set times such as lesson bells, television programmes, shop opening hours, break and lunch times, even church service times, for example, that I fail to see the opportunities offered by unforseen, even unwelcome, events. This is not a good thing as it limits my chances to experience God working in unexpected ways. For all of us the predictions, forecasts and plans we have thrust upon our days bring the risk that we may become too blinkered to see, sense and even feel God's presence.

The watercolour, of the scene in the Cornish churchyard at Landewednack, with a beautiful splash of colour, reflects for me how God steals into our affairs in the most unexpected ways. Suddenly we are aware of his presence as he 'breaks through' and often 'hits us'. It may happen in church on Sunday but more often it is somewhere completely unexpected. It may take place at any time, at home, in the town or in the country, at a family event or with friends. We may be viewing a rainbow after a summer shower, walking through bluebells, or crunching through snow as we are forced to walk to work in the winter. It may be as we enjoy the splendour of a coastal view or the peaceful atmosphere of a churchyard. It may simply occur viewing a robin on a fence.

Such awe-inspiring beauty is fragile, for it doesn't stay long and we cannot take it with us. Like everything, it becomes one of many experiences as we deepen our personal relationship with an unpredictable God. There are so many occasions in the Gospels when we hear that the disciples were so unprepared for what happened that they missed the beauty, significance or real meaning of it; so often they were surprised and didn't seem to know how to respond. Amidst all the business of life, amidst all our planning for the future, we need to watch and listen for God's presence. He needs us to be flexible enough to respond to his unexpected working.

Can you recall unexpected events that have brought new challenges and opportunities?

How can we learn to see God working in our lives, in the people we meet, and in the things we see and do?

19

Alba

Chapter Six

Once, on a Geography fieldcourse to Germany, we stayed in the beautifully quaint town of Boppard, located in the Rhine Gorge. Travelling along the Rhine and Mosel Valleys we couldn't help but notice that every conceivable inch of hillside was covered with vineyards, even the steepest slopes.

In March, when the fieldcourse took place, the terraces looked to be covered with sticks - seemingly lifeless pieces of stalk, admittedly carefully pruned, tapered and fixed but looking dead nonetheless. Seeing the watercolour of Alba, in south west France, for the first time, I was reminded of this stark German landscape, even though, in Alba, the picture shows only a small plot of vines on the outskirts of the village.

On closer inspection, these apparently dead stalks are full of shoots near the base. Within a couple of months the fields will be covered with green vines. The life cycle has begun again and our trip to the winery demonstrated this. On the slopes of the Rhine Gorge, volcanic soils and sheltered south-facing slopes which catch the sun and protect the fruit are the basis from which, in August and September, the grapes are harvested, pressed and matured to produce wine. Visiting the vineyards, as we did, studying the processes involved and seeing these empty looking terraces it is difficult to imagine such a new cycle. Yet the wine cellars, full of quality wines, are evidence of its success.

At school I am constantly reminded of this idea of a cycle of development. Students enter the school, pass through the different stages of growing up (and all that that entails!) and, very quickly, it seems, leave us to follow a career or study at university. Our mission statement reminds us that we aim to provide students with the qualities and qualifications required to make their way in the world. Every one is unique, every one is an individual and it quickly becomes apparent that our students make their own way through the cycle.

Unfortunately some students veer off course and lose their way completely. Others change course for various reasons, maybe a family problem or change in circumstance, or probably a personal urge to do something different, to try something new. I remember one student surprising everyone by announcing that he wanted a break from A Level routine to join an Adventure Camp in the United States providing holiday fun for disabled and disadvantaged children from the cities of New York State. Another decided, halfway through some very successful examination studies, to quit and find work on a farm in New Zealand.

All these remind me of the beginning of one of my favourite stories, Kenneth Graham's unforgettable tale, *The Wind in the Willows*. Mole is doing some spring cleaning 'till he has dust in his throat and eyes and splashes of whitewash all over his fur, an aching back and weary arms.' But this particular spring there was pressure on him, 'a spirit of divine discontent and longing', which led him to do something different, to fling down his brush and bolt out of his little home.

To Mole this was a new experience. Being outside by the riverbank, in the meadows and country lanes, among the flowers and wild wood was a whole new existence and all these were to become part of his new world. To Mole, spring cleaning was part of his dull and boring routine which was becoming a strain and he was longing for a change. Discontent eventually led him to dash down his tunnel into the springtime and daylight. The story is full of his adventures.

This idea of new life, symbolised by a vine, is an interesting one and is very common in the New Testament. It can become a useful signpost for our walk. To begin to find God's tracks and walk in faith is definitely to participate in something new. Paul, writing in a letter to the newly established Christian Church in Colossae, emphasises the same message, a message of commitment to become 'new' people created to be like Jesus Christ, walking in a new light and not in the old darkness, living in faith and love.

C. S. Lewis tells us, in his book *Surprised by Joy*, that while he was travelling in a sidecar of a motorcycle en route to Whipsnade Zoo, something exciting happened to him. He says that when he set out he didn't believe that Jesus was the Son of God and when he reached the zoo he did. He wasn't aware of why this change came about but he writes, 'It was more like a man, after a long sleep, still lying motionless in bed, becoming aware that he is now awake'. There he must have stood, in Whipsnade Zoo, on the threshold of new, exciting and challenging adventures, the like of which he hadn't dreamed of before.

It all seems sudden and drastic and in a sense it was, although he had been deepening his faith for some time. There is no doubt, however, that this was a big change from his negative attitude to the Christianity of his childhood days. Even in the late 1920s he may have believed in God, a power outside of himself, but it was not until that journey in a sidecar to the safari park that he actually believed that the Gospel story was true and that Jesus was the Son of God.

This theme of new life is certainly exciting, but it is also challenging and uncertain as C. S. Lewis often told us. The vines planted in the plot on the outskirts of Alba look dead but actually they are not. New shoots begin new life. Whatever we think, walking along one of God's tracks is going to prove different.

In Isaiah we read that 'whether you turn to the right or to the left, your ears will hear a voice behind you, saying, 'This is the way; walk in it.' (Isaiah 30:21). Have you ever expeienced a change in the direction of your life? Did you feel that God's hand was in the change? How did you know?

How satisfied are you with life? Try asking God to help you see everyday experiences in a different way. Think of each one as an opportunity to show how much God means to you.

Chapter Seven

Rereading the late Stuart Blanch's book *Living by Faith* a few months ago brought home to me how faith can be tested even in the most ordinary aspects of everyday life. He begins his book by highlighting our daily expression of faith in people, machines and procedures. He writes that he believes, though he cannot prove it, that when he catches the train to London, the track workers have done their job, the mechanics have tested the wheels, the signals are working, the engine driver is sober and indeed every train driver in every other train in the system is sober too. This, Blanch highlights, is a massive act of faith which he shares with his fellow travellers as they eat breakfast and read the newspapers together.

Faith is fragile for I reread this only days before the Hatfield rail disaster in which people died and many were seriously injured because, so we understand, of faulty tracking. Such a tragedy rocks our faith. From personal experience I know that such events do this. A close clergy friend of our family, living in Sowerby Bridge, West Yorkshire, had a neighbour, who one morning was walking to the local post office. As a young mum she had her toddler twins with her. The post office was situated on the main road into the town. In the next few seconds a lorry veered out of control, careered down the steep hill and ploughed into the front window of the post office, killing the mum.

Every time we get into a train, or go out shopping, or see a doctor or take our car to the garage for a service, we put faith in people, machines and procedures. Fortunately this faith is rarely misplaced. When it is, though, the consequences can be very serious and sometimes tragic.

This faith, however, is different to the faith by which Paul lived and by which he wanted all Christians to live. He became so frustrated by people who looked for signs, proof or complicated, watertight arguments before they would believe in Jesus. You can imagine Paul, by his own admission a person with few debating skills, trying to persuade both Jews and Gentiles to live by the faith of Jesus that so dominated his life.

Reference to watertight arguments reminds me of the story of two men discussing their faith. One of them remarked:

'I don't have anything to do with things I don't understand.'

'Have you had breakfast?', asked the other.

'Yes!', said the first, 'but what has that got to do with it?'

'Did you have butter on your toast?' persisted his friend.

'Yes', replied the man, increasingly bewildered.

'Well can you tell me how a black and white cow eating green grass can make white milk which is turned into yellow butter?'

'No, I can't', admitted the sceptic.

'Well', his friend advised, 'I wouldn't have anything to do with breakfast either.'

Our interestingly striking watercolour, in this chapter, is of a rural French scene, entitled the Goats and Geese at Gras. It is interesting because my eyes take me from the open field full of grazing goats along the curved street, lined with trees and vivid colour roofs, to the church, on top of the hill. From wherever I start in the painting my eyes tend to be drawn to the church at the top of the hill. I try to imagine how the church must have dominated village life for generations, and how it still does, being a central and moulding force to shape village patterns and individual decisions of faith. There are no watertight arguments or signs for proof here.

On a grander scale William Golding, in his novel *The Spire*, takes his readers back to medieval times and relives the pressures and challenges of building a cathedral tower. Rising above all the tensions between the people involved in its construction, the tower gradually begins to dominate the local scene and remoulds the surrounding landscape as people, from everywhere around, became affected by the pulling power of the cathedral and its tower, carving out new paths across the landscape to reach it. The attraction was something more than a complicated argument. It did not provide proof of faith either. The village church, in the watercolour of Alba, may have been less complicated and frustrating to build but its significance is evident nonetheless.

Jesus had to face people who wanted proof of who he was and where he came from, who demanded that he perform miracles, who asked him awkward questions and tried to trick him. Even when he was on the cross, the Jewish rulers wanted him to prove himself by saving himself. Doubting Thomas, too, wanted proof of the resurrection. All Jesus wanted was that people believe in him and in his Father.

At school I feel good when I am able to believe in students and be part of the important turning points in their lives. On many occasions I misunderstand or fail to understand their thoughts and actions. Sometimes I disagree with them. As a teacher it is a privilege to be an influence on them as they develop confidence in themselves as individuals. Jesus also took every opportunity to make his disciples think and to deepen their faith in him. We have to realise that there is more to faith than just making an initial decision. One of George Appleton's *Jerusalem Prayers* is a great one to use:

O God, I could not begin to seek you, if you had not sought me and made yourself known to me first. Now I want to know you more truly, deeply and intuitively and to discover more about you. I will seek until I find, knock at your door until you open to me, ask until I receive the gift of yourself, O God, my God.

Our walk with God ought to be changing and shaping us. That may sound frightening or even dramatic. No one has all the answers. Sometimes a meaningful Christian response to events is far from easy, but without it there is no point in tracing tracks across our beach.

Read Hebrews 12:1, 2. Sometimes it really is difficult to start living by faith or to hang on by faith. What practical help have you found in such situations? How does it help to 'fix our eyes on Jesus', and know that he endured everything, even death on a cross?

Look at Matthew 7:24-27. Is your life firmly built on the words of Jesus and your response to them?

La Roche, Alba.

Chapter Eight

The inscription on the birthday card from one of my daughters stated that I am now a person who really stands out in a crowd - of young people! My other daughter's card, the same year, claimed that I shouldn't worry about getting older, because when people ask where her good looks come from she will always say - from Mum! Reading these reminded me, again, of my growing number of grey hairs and receding hair style. Whatever I think, though, I cannot start again. None of us can.

On our Christian walk, however, things are different. When we first become Christians we are born again, so Jesus says, by the Holy Spirit. God becomes our Father. Even if we later make a mess of things, we can be forgiven and move forward. We can go back to the beginning and start again. Whether it is our first or thousandth attempt at following God's tracks, our Father in heaven will not give up on us. Paul emphasises this, writing that we are renewed each day and that instead of regretting lost opportunities and past failures we should be concentrating on each day and what it brings.

My choice of the scene at La Roche, Alba, as a watercolour to accompany this chapter may seem strange. To me it captures an everyday scene, perhaps a lunchtime in a rural, quiet and unhurried village. Lifestyles are traditional, maintained as time goes by. Lives in such a setting are shaped by experiences, by the people encountered, by the challenges and opportunities offered within this local context. Farmers or gardeners tend their vines and vegetables, house-keepers look proudly to their chores, shopkeepers are keen to while away their day gossiping to customers in shop doorways. Time almost seems to stand still.

This scene is a million miles away from a lunchtime in school. As the bell sounds for its end, the rush is on. Scruffy boys with their shirts hanging out and shoes or trainers covered in mud after playing football are herded along the corridors and upstairs to registration. It is pandemonium. The talk is not gossip, it is of lost goal-scoring chances, worries about being unprepared for the French test in the afternoon lesson, and the boring assembly time to come.

In each case, though, personalities are being formed, shaped by everyday experiences, events and people encountered. Just as with the lives of those villagers, so too with school pupils and with Christian disciples. And the remarkable thing for us Christians is that Jesus said that he would be with us, where we are now, in what we are doing now. It is no good looking for him anywhere else.

In his book *Friendship with God* David Hope, the Archbishop of York, reminds us that each day is a gift from God which holds out immense opportunities for us, the first day of the rest of our lives - whatever happened yesterday or will happen tomorrow. These words strike a chord with me. Another reference I often use is the anonymous poem, quoted by Selwyn Hughes in his book *Understanding the Presence of God*:

> Every morning lean thine arm awhile
> Upon the window sill of heaven
> And gaze upon thy God
> Then with the vision in thy heart
> Turn strong to meet the day.

This poem tells me much about the priorities I should have. Those all-too-rare, still moments with God at the beginning of the day are priceless because quiet prayer gives us the strength to face whatever may occur. Each day, at home and school, I find out that a busy life takes unexpected turns. We need, therefore, to gaze upon God each morning, and take his vision away with us to face our day, whatever it may entail.

While on holiday in the Netherlands two years ago we took the opportunity of visiting Corrie Ten Boom's house and watchmaker's shop in Haarlem. Looking down at the hustle and bustle of a very busy street we stood cheek by jowl in the Hiding Place and imagined as best we could the situation when six Jews stood in that hole the size of a wardrobe, for several days, hiding from the Gestapo. The visit made me read some more of Corrie's work written over almost forty years of Christian devotion, a devotion that led her from the horrors of Ravensbruck concentration camp to 'tramp' around the world spreading the Christian message. In her book *Clippings from My Notebook* she outlines her strongly-held beliefs. I want to quote three *clippings*:

I believe that we are often failure conscious. Faith makes us victory conscious. Faith brings the unreality of hope to the reality of now. Hope is future. Faith is present. Faith is the radar that shows us the reality of Christ's victory.

Let us not underestimate the power and work of the Holy Spirit. To be 'born again' means not only our turning to God, but God's putting His Spirit within us to be the new life in our souls, thus making us children of God.

The Holy Spirit does not tell us that we are strong or that we can do anything or everything if we have positive thinking. That is pure fantasy. The Holy Spirit tells us that we are nothing in ourselves. We are like gloves that are filled with a hand and that hand is the Holy Spirit.

Earlier we said that, on our beach, we have to face decisions. Sometimes these decisions are simple while at other times they are almost impossible to make. Such decisions occur daily. We may find God every day in each of the situations we face. Jesus tells us we have the help of the Holy Spirit and, as Corrie reminds us, we must not underestimate his power as we walk with him and grow in faith.

Do you sometimes feel that most days start with thoughts about yesterday's problems? I know this is often true for me. But in the book of Lamentations we are told this: 'Because of the LORD's great love we are not consumed, for his compassions never fail. They are new every morning. Great is your faithfulness.' (Lamentations 3:22, 23). Be encouraged by these words.

Have you talked much to God about your faith? Who and what are the influences on your faith? How is the Holy Spirit helping you to grow in faith?

31

A street
in Vogue

La Roche

Chapter Nine

Returning to the theme of turning points, we know that any one of these involves a change of direction. Imagine standing in the small village square depicted in our next watercolour. Look towards the church. Do we turn and walk down the lane on the left or turn right into the doorway? Do we walk straight on, round the steps and through the arched gateway or climb up and over the steps? Whatever the decision, it will involve a change in direction and some sense of mystery.

Turning points are as familiar to teachers as they are to parents. Although thrilling and exciting to be an influence on students' development, it is also challenging, as they move (or sometimes lurch) from one turning point to another. Throughout both primary school and secondary school there are so many turning points. Being both teacher and parent, I have been part of many. I see changes from exchange of swap cards to concert tickets; from bringing a pedal bicycle to a car to school, (often newer and in much better condition than most staff cars!); from keen youngsters muddying their shoes playing football, through Year 11 students keen to wear their shirts outside their trousers and reveal a macho image to spotty but sophisticated Sixth Formers all too eager to grow up quickly.

It has been amusingly said that easily recognisable turning points for parents include the time when they can no longer help with their children's homework, the time when the car their children want doesn't come from a toy shop, and the time when children request a loan rather than pocket money. Finally comes the time when their daughter remarks, 'My mum wants me to accompany her on a trip around the world but I want to go somewhere else', and their son says to the shop assistant, 'Is it possible to bring this shirt back if my mother likes it?'

There are more serious turning points that involve making some major decisions about commitment to work, attitudes, values, behaviour and responsibility. What courses do I follow at GCSE or A level? Do I go to university or try for a career straightaway? How best do I handle this crisis in my relationship with my parents? If my friend is leaving school at 16, do I? What happens when my girlfriend and I have ended our relationship? What do I do when one of my best friends asks me to try some cannabis or to cover for him as he steals from another member of the tutor group? How do I react now that I know that my mum is dying of cancer? It's all part of growing up – making new friends, developing relationships, taking examinations, passing tests, taking up new opportunities and new challenges – turning corners.

When former students come back to school, I realise how going to university, leaving home, starting a job, being in a serious relationship, having children, are all turning points. Richard, whom we met in the first chapter, showed this to me. Some of his turning points were totally unexpected. The sudden and unexpected death of the father of a student only five months after the student had left our school to study French at university, shows how unexpected turning points can happen. All of them mean uncertainty, sometimes frighteningly so. But they can often be exhilarating and exciting experiences too.

However, they all create new situations, new opportunities and new problems.

In leaving behind the family carpenter's shop in Nazareth and his home, family and friends, to concentrate on a public ministry in Galilee, Jesus experienced his first of many turning points. His baptism in the River Jordan, and the temptations he faced in the desert, were others. The beginning of relationships with his disciples and the loss of some of his friends such as Lazarus are points with which we can identify as well. Jesus' decision to go to Jerusalem, knowing that he would be killed, was perhaps his biggest turning point. Although we face very different turning points, the challenges and the implications are just as real to us.

The important influence of others is also evident in Jesus' experiences. At Caesarea Philippi Jesus faced perhaps his most important decision. In prayerful discussion he asks his disciples a searching question: 'Who do people say I am?' The disciples seemed to find the answer easy: 'Some say John the Baptist, others say Elijah, and still others, one of the prophets.' Quickly came a follow-up question which stunned his friends into silence: 'But who do you say I am?' It was Peter who spoke up: 'You are the Christ, the Son of the Living God' (Matthew 16:16). That was the answer Jesus was looking for. He knew that their faith was weak, but they knew who he was and were prepared to own up to it. This must have given him extra resolve to travel on to Jerusalem and face that final stage of his ministry.

If you have come across those magic eye pictures which create 3D images from a mass of continuous and confusing patterns, you will know that if you relax your eyes and stare into the picture you will see a 3D image standing out of these repetitive patterns. Once you begin to relax and stare into a page of seemingly meaningless patterns, you begin a voyage of discovery to find a hidden picture full of unexpected clarity and incredible detail.

I think this is true for the experiences along our walk of faith. For the disciples, proclaiming their belief in Jesus at Caesarea Philippi was only a beginning. What Jesus spoke about and the events that followed made everything very confusing. Yet the rest of their lives would be spent discovering the hidden detail of what this belief meant. Their walk in faith opened up new perspectives of a living and caring God. It happened with C. S. Lewis, after his visit to the safari park, as he was able to arrive at a new and much deeper faith. Does it happen to us as we turn our corners and develop new relationships? We get to know others and influence them as they experience their own personal turning points. Through these experiences and our prayers we get to know Jesus too.

Have you experienced turning points in your life through which you have come to know Jesus or to have a closer relationship with him?

'Trust in the LORD with all your heart and lean not on your own understanding; in all your ways acknowledge him and he will direct your paths' (Proverbs 3:5, 6). How can doing this make a difference to the way we make decisions?

Church Cove
Landewednack

Chapter ten

As you look at the watercolour of a Cornish coastal scene selected for this chapter, your eyes follow the long winding way gradually moving from sea to shore, from boat to car, from village to countryside, from the known and easily perceived to the unknown way as it bends around the hill and over the horizon. It is a peaceful, idyllic scene. The road is quiet, but like most roads it is full of different perspectives, changes of direction and new aspects.

It is experience of such changes which makes a walk along God's tracks so challenging. Yes, we know that Jesus told us that he is with us always. Our tracks, however, are not always peaceful and idyllic. We have to travel up slope and down slope, and some of the slopes are very steep indeed. When the track disappears round a corner we may feel very uncertain.

Do you have a day, important in your memory, which you will never forget? I do. It was one of those days when the unthinkable happens. My second daughter had been born on the Friday, 21st March, and our spring had started

beautifully. It had been a wonderful moment when the newest member of our family came home from hospital on Palm Sunday. The rest of the Geography staff and other teachers, including the Deputy Head, were in the Netherlands on a fieldcourse.

On Monday, winds of over 100 miles uprooted a 60ft sycamore tree at our school, and sent it crashing down onto a classroom of students in the middle of a lesson. Firemen battled for more than twenty minutes to free Michael but he was dead on arrival at the hospital. Miraculously only two other boys were hurt, though not seriously, in this freak accident. Tragically the school lost one of its most popular Sixth Formers.

The event, which happened in seconds, was a stunning blow. Boys openly wept for Michael; it was that awkwardness with words, people not knowing what to say, what to do, which said it all. The group abroad heard about the tragedy, almost immediately, on the news. They felt awkward too.

I taught Michael. It wasn't long before the tragedy that we were talking of the coursework he was planning and the last football match in which he had played. He was a talented cricketer too. I knew what he was like. I knew that the words of the Headmaster's reading were particularly poignant. Normally boys hardly take it in, they don't really want to listen. This year was different, for the words took on a new significance: 'Father, into your hands I commit my spirit!' 'Jesus said this and died'.

An incident like this is certainly a test of faith. Over one summer a few years ago three members of our staff died in totally unrelated circumstances, and that was a real test. One died of cancer, one in a horrific road accident while riding his bicycle, and one from pneumonia. These events shocked a small and close-knit staff, creating great anxiety about the future and about the meaning of faith. Having a very close relative suffering and dying from cancer is also truly a test of faith. The ups and downs and bends in the road in our watercolour remind me that the feel-good days and precious friendships are inter-spersed with disappointments, loneliness, pain, and fear of what the future may hold.

Michael died in Holy Week, which in some ways made his death even more poignant. We were reminded of how Jesus told his disciples that he would soon leave them to prepare a way ahead for them. He promised to return again and assured them that, in time, they would see the way ahead for themselves. Meanwhile they should not worry, but trust in God and in Jesus himself.

Thomas would have spoken for all the disciples and for many of us when he said, 'Lord, we don't know where you are going, so how can we know the way?' A logical question, it seems, in the circumstances. Everything had become very confusing and complicated and the disciples were being told not to worry, but to trust that they would be shown the right way forward. When something like Michael's death or a loved one's suffering occurs, it is difficult to see any way ahead and even more difficult to trust.

Jesus' answer to Thomas' question was: 'I am the Way, the Truth and the Life.' In the assembly following Michael's death it was difficult to put these words of Jesus into context. When we thought of Michael's parents and of Michael's dreams and aspirations for his future, as well as of the turning points he had experienced at school already, it was indeed difficult. Yet Jesus was telling the greatest truth of all to a band of ordinary, very frightened men, huddled together in an upper room, wondering what was happening, what was about to happen and where they would go from here. To them it seemed to make no sense. Why then? Why them? Why at all? Early in that Holy Week when Michael died, as on many other occasions, perhaps we knew how they felt.

Jesus says, 'I am the Way', the way to God, the way to first glimpse God then to get to know him and understand what he is really like. In those first days after Michael's death, with all the sadness and confusion, anxiety and disillusionment, I felt God's presence more than ever. I felt my faith strengthen and I felt as though I

came face to face with the cross. Jesus' disciples must have felt demoralised in the upper room in Jerusalem when Jesus said that he was leaving them. When he said, 'Come now, let us leave', they knew they had to go, they had to turn a corner, as it were, on the road out of Jerusalem, and face uncertainty. This would be a walk in faith, but they seemed at peace, knowing that Jesus was with them as their companion. They didn't need maps or directions. They had a personal guide.

Is there a day or an event that you will never forget? Was your faith strengthened or are you still struggling with questions about it? If you are struggling, try reading the first six verses of Psalm 37.

John tells us in his Gospel that when Thomas, one of the disciples, heard of Jesus's resurrection, he doubted that it had taken place and wanted proof (John 20:24-31). Meeting the risen Jesus changed his attitude. Does Thomas's openness help you with your faith?

La Roche

Cottage at Colquinth

Chapter Eleven

I have always enjoyed gardens and the countryside. I am not a keen gardener myself but enjoy the results of other people's work. Whenever I look at a garden, whether it be a cottage garden set in idyllic surroundings like the one in our next watercolour or the garden of a stately home, it always seems to reveal beauty and wonder but also a sense of incompleteness, of mystery and constant change. These sentiments make the watercolour come alive, the splashes and different shades of colour capturing the atmosphere well. The complexity of brush strokes seems to reveal a mixture of order and mystery as seen in the splendour of God's creation but portrayed in the smallness of a Cornish cottage garden.

These feelings come across in Frances Hodgson Burnett's story of *The Secret Garden:*

> And then she took a long breath and looked behind her up the long walk to see if anyone was coming… she held back the swinging curtain of ivy and pushed back the door which opened slowly. Then she slipped through it and shut it behind her and stood with her back against it looking about her and breathing quite fast with excitement and wonder and delight. She was standing in the secret garden.

The girl is Mary Lennox, a spoilt, selfish girl sent to live with her uncle in Yorkshire. She finds her way into a secret garden, previously known only to her dead mother and aunt. Discovering it, together with a local boy and her sickly cousin, changes their lives. There is, in every sense, wonder and joy at the changing seasonal nature of the beautiful garden, feelings of love and mystery in connection with their dead mother and aunt, and the wonderful incompleteness and unpredictability of a story kept hidden for so long.

These feelings can, of course, be experienced in many situations. We do not have to be peering over a cottage garden wall or entering a secret garden to be awe-inspired or to be surrounded by a sense of love. We can all think, I'm sure, of moments when we sensed joy and love, or of

people we know (or have known) who radiated a sense of God's presence. We can experience God's splendour and his beautiful love through nature but even more through the people we meet. As we reflected in the last chapter, it is in looking at God's love, face to face with Jesus on the Cross, that we become those who can also reflect it in our suffering world.

Sarah was one of those people who radiated God's love. She was a great teacher, one of the best. When she came to our school as a young mathematician we knew she was special because of the way she related to her students. She showed a remarkable care for them as individuals much wider than just helping them with their algebra or statistics. She became very popular. She started up a drama club and, within what seemed a short time, we were watching a polished performance of a West End musical. She took on a major pastoral role, yet no problem was too small. Thinking of her, I call to mind our cottage garden for one of her ideas was to introduce a gardening club to help bring some life and colour to a very drab school exterior. An

exciting pond project was the immediate result.

Not long after arriving at our school Sarah experienced an unhappy divorce and took on the responsibility of bringing up her son on her own. Yet it was Sarah who set up theatre and concert visits for staff, who had time for everyone and who gained some of the best results for her subject. Sarah was the face and the presence which seemed to make it all worthwhile.

It was a terrific shock to be told one day that she had been diagnosed with secondary stomach cancer. She had fought cancer for some time but we knew that this time it was serious. The end was quite quick. Not long before she died she came in with her youngster, still smiling, oozing that sense of God's caring love. The students crowded round her determined to make sure that she felt at home. The news of her death, although expected, was met with total shock. The school closed for a day and so many students and staff wanted to be at the service that it had to be relayed outside the church. It was an incredible day. Sarah was an incredible person.

The apostle John, in his Gospel, writes about the God of love, a love by which we give of ourselves to others, which is an essential part of our Christian walk. How can we, though, accept that, with all our pains and illnesses, frustrations and feelings of inadequacy, heartbreaks and failings, we can make the slightest difference? Paul, in his first epistle to the Corinthians, lists qualities of Christian love. He includes patience and generosity, kindness and humility, courtesy and honesty. Sarah showed us that these qualities are real. She had a faith, although she didn't go to church much, and she showed it by walking in this love and illustrated that the way of love creates the very nature of our tracks.

It is no good waiting for the right time or place or waiting until we are ready. We may lose the opportunity. In a way it is quite frightening that Jesus, in claiming that God is love, gave us all a choice – accept it and enjoy it, use it and live by it or leave it alone. There is the joy, mystery, wonder and challenge of our faith, all in one. The watercolour of the Cornish cottage and its garden wonderfully reveals the splendour of God's beautiful creation. Gardens can, of course, be drab and colourless, untidy and wild. No garden stays the same or is ever perfect. But each of us is invited to open the door into our secret garden and to identify the true mystery of God's love for us. It is never complete, and it is unpredictable. But it is there for us to experience forever.

Thank God for any places, people or circumstances which have helped you experience the love and splendour of God.

Ask God to help you reflect more and more in the things you do each day the quality of love (1 Corinthians 13:4-7).

Charles
(Retired Postman)
of Alba.

Chapter twelve

Talking with people as they study Graham Clake's watercolour of Charles in his potting shed, it is interesting that so many different perspectives emerge as they describe how the scene 'speaks' to them. Some focus on the plants, some on Charles himself and some on the context of the location. Personally, I find the watercolour portrays a picture of contentment. Charles, retired from his job as a postman in Alba, France, potters about among his plants, relaxed and unrushed, happy with what he is doing and with life. This is important, as happiness is an important aspect of our tracks across the beach. Why should we feel guilty about trying to find it?

The Jerusalem Bible translates Paul's words to the Philippian church like this: 'I want you to be happy, always happy in the Lord... what I want is your happiness.' This is a statement all the more incredible as he was being held a prisoner at the time, humiliated at the hands of the Romans. Yet he claims that, deep inside himself, he is content and joyful and it is this inner contentment that he wants others to share.

This inner contentment seems to be an essential ingredient. Being happy can sometimes be shallow and a smile can hide many feelings. From experience, I know that we often try to create happiness to hide anxiety, suffering, even grief underneath.

Darren, a second year Sixth Form student entered school one morning last term and caused quite a stir. He was really happy. Donning a leopard skin hairstyle (blonde with large black spots), he quickly gained attention from his friends. Darren is noted for his individuality; on charity non-uniform days he wears his skate boarding or roller skating gear, but this seemed extreme even for him and on a normal day! He laughed and joked with friends and my instant reaction, as Head of his Year group, was to put an immediate end to his fun!

In my office, before I was allowed to begin my pre-prepared onslaught, he burst into tears. It wasn't so much that he was worried about what I might do, although Darren's first words were: 'I know I have done wrong but you see....' The story behind his behaviour this particular morning concerned Tim, his best friend from outside school. The two of them had planned a Kenyan safari in July 2001 after their A Levels and they decided that, just before they were to go they would dye their hair to match the local wildlife. A few days before his 'shock' entry into school Tim had been diagnosed with a rare form of cancer in the upper bone marrow of his legs. After many tests and several different opinions came this devastating news for these friends. Darren was heartbroken and had decided to bring forward his hair colouring to coincide with a visit to his friend at a London hospital. Knowing that Tim had been informed of the seriousness of his cancer Darren was happy that morning knowing that he had made a positive decision to make his friend feel good.

Such outward happiness can hide so much. As we watch a very close relative suffer terminal cancer, my family know how it feels. This transient happiness is all too easily experienced too when we open a present we really want, share a meal with family or friends or enjoy some hot, sunny weather which makes us feel good about ourselves.

True joy seems a rarer experience. Yet Paul claims it to be part of the fruit of the Spirit along with love, peace, patience, kindness, humility, faithfulness, goodness and self control. It is meant to be central in a Christian's life, enriching not only our own lives but also those around us.

Sometimes, though, the experience of joy does become ordinary and predictable as we confuse transient happiness with true joy. It is inner joy which comes from the hidden strength and power of Jesus. This, to Paul, overrode all his pain and suffering, all his disappointment and failure.

Everywhere, on our Christian walk too, there is evidence of people's faith in God, illustrated by experience. And with each experience comes a deep and everlasting joy and inner happiness which is reflected in laughter and contentment. Although we are never told that Jesus laughed, only that he wept, it is hard to imagine that thousands of people would flock to hear parables, stories and teachings, to be healed and comforted, from a boring, miserable and uninteresting person.

Time, place or context seem unimportant. The most unexpected circumstances, even of extreme suffering and patience, can lead to the sense of real Christian joy and nothing can take this away. In the book *Great Hymns and their Stories* by W.J. Limmer Sheppard, we read that it was while alone, during a period of sorrow after the break up of his engagement, and a recent bereavement that the words came to blind George Matheson to write the inspired hymn 'O Love that wilt not let me go'. One summer evening in 1882, while he was sitting at his manse in Innellan, Argyllshire he wrote:

> O Joy that seekest me through pain,
> I cannot close my heart to Thee,
> I trace the rainbow through the rain,
> And feel the promise is not in vain,
> That morn shall tearless be.

It is interesting that just before Christmas I spoke again to Darren. We laughed about the leopard skin haircut. He seemed relaxed and more confident. He had every reason to be. Tim had responded well to treatment. He may not be going to walk properly for a long time, if ever, but there is every chance, so the doctors say, that he will survive the cancer. There was an inner contentment that showed through Darren. We haven't talked about his faith, though perhaps there will be an opportunity for this in the near future. But Christians reflect this contentment through a faith in Jesus, and I reminded myself of Peter's words, in his first Epistle, 'Cast all your anxieties on him because he cares for you'. The alternative to excessive and negative worry, interspersed with glimpses of happiness, is to trust in a God who cares and to live one step at a time.

Jesus says: 'I have come that they may have life, and have it to the full' (John 10:10). Do you feel that you have an inner contentment? Are you usually 'happy in the Lord'? Thank God that what he wants for you is 'life to the full.'

How can prayer help us find inner contentment (Philippians 4:6, 7)?

windmill
at
Icklesham
nr, merricks

Chapter Thirteen

If we were asked to describe our favourite dream landscape we would, I'm sure, all come up with different ideas. My dreamscape would not be too dissimilar to our next watercolour. The picture, of Ickenham windmill, contains lots of green and open spaces, hills and open roads, a quiet, peaceful, unpolluted landscape lit up by a full moon and dominated by a symbol of God's energy, the windmill. It reminds me of fieldwork landscapes from university, of scenes from family holidays we have shared and of landscapes I came to know as a boy in rural Northamptonshire. Your dreamscape is, more than likely, going to be different. Possibly you will think of sun-drenched beaches and palm trees, of mountain peaks and glaciers, of art galleries and street cafes. Whatever our dreamscape includes, it is healthy to dream.

Our dreams are not going to be dramatic. No dreamscape can be simpler than a windmill on the top of a hill and many of my dreams are simple too. Our response to our dreams is not going to set the world on fire, either. But when we dream God's dreams they should lead to a celebration of life and faith, of what God has created for us, in us and other people - a celebration of growth in fellowship and friendship, of love and service.

Celebrating our positive achievements and those of other people is very important in our walk of faith. We all want our efforts to be celebrated, and this is especially true of youngsters as they grow up. That is why it is such an important part of school life. Students who perceive that they achieve nothing worth celebrating perceive wrongly. All students, even those whom teachers find it extremely difficult to contemplate joining in a celebration for, deserve celebration for something in their lives.

When Mark actually understands a piece of mathematics homework for the first time, when Richard begins to improve his writing, when Alex manages, for the first time, to stay in school for the whole day without becoming upset and wanting to go home, when George succeeds in getting the Sixth Form to raise a lot of money for a local children's hospice by organising a rendition of the popular TV programme 'Stars in their Eyes' and charging the students for the privilege of enjoying it, it is time to celebrate. All these celebrations count. Those words of praise or thanks, encouragement or support, the piece of work displayed, the written congratulatory note, the celebratory event; all these are part of a celebration of life at school.

My windmill dreamscape is full of the celebration of God's beauty, of his love and care for us, of his energy and power. It reflects his glory. So too will your dreamscape, whatever its focus. And that is what our walk is all about. Yet we are bound to meet people on our journey of faith who claim that Christian love is an irrelevant dream that can never begin to become reality.

As we journey we need to dream. For example, I would love to reach a situation where all the class are interested in my subject, where they work hard and learn to imagine a world of unpolluted air and clean streets, of roads with no traffic jams, of undisturbed wildernesses and unspoilt gardens. I dream that they can then go home to a safe and caring neighbourhood, where they have no opportunity to be involved in crime or drugs. I dream, too, that they will, in their own time and way, begin a Christian walk along the tracks on their own beach.

Celebration is, I believe, a way of making dreams happen. Through our dreams we can thank God for what he gives us and begin to discover the real link between our faith and our community, our friends and family, our work place, our leisure time and our world.

Christianity is firmly rooted in our world. And what is the point of having a faith if we cannot dream of how to use it? This, as always, is the challenge. How far are we prepared to pray and work to make our dreams come true? And how concerned are we to encourage those we know, especially young people, to dare to dream and to make a difference in the world? All it may take to help somone to start walking this path may be some words of encouragement, thanks and praise.

Paul writes to the believers at Philippi that he thanks God every time he remembers them. He prays for them with joy because of their partnership in the gospel, confident that God is working through them (Philippians 1:3-6). How important is it for us to encourage and thank others?

Do you regularly thank God for his gifts to you, for your achievements and successes and the things that make you feel good? How can we add more celebration to our lives?

Paul writes that God 'is able to do immeasurably more than all we ask or imagine, according to his power that is at work within us' (Ephesians 3:20). In the light of this promise, bring to God some of your unfulfilled dreams, and ask him to do something that will make you truly glad.

FE118 at Dungeness

Chapter Fourteen

While a Sixth Form tutor I had a phone call one day that really worried me. It was a Thursday in October and the call was from Stephen's Mum. He was a student in my group and had walked out of home the night before leaving a note informing his Mum that he needed to get away from everything and everyone. Stephen was a sensitive and intelligent student, popular with his peers and on his way towards three good A level grades. I had been forewarned about this news by one of Stephen's anxious friends but it was a shock all the same. To increase his Mum's stress his best friend had committed suicide the previous year and Stephen's parents had split up during the summer. He lived with his Mum and only saw his Dad at specific weekends. The situation definitely could not have been worse.

Fortunately Stephen returned very late on Thursday and was back in school on Friday. Why? Because his two best friends went out of school and found him. They spent all day and most of the night finding him, talking to him and bringing him home. It wasn't his parents or myself, as form tutor, that did it, although we had all spent time over recent weeks talking to him about his feelings, his problems and his aspirations. He had good friends, the very best.

This incident made me think of Jesus' words recorded in John's Gospel. Jesus claims that the greatest thing anyone can do is to love one another and the greatest love a person can have for his friends is to give his life for them. Stephen's friends did not have to do what they did but they spent time looking and when they found him they brought him home. Jesus says that if we do what he commands us to do and love one another, then we can become his friends. What an incredible invitation!

Andrew and John's callings, to be Jesus' disciples were as an answer to a similar invitation. They asked Jesus where he lived and immediately Jesus says: 'Come and see'. They spent the rest of the day with him. How extraordinary to be invited to spend a day with Jesus! Imagine, it would be like meeting a friend. Such a friendship with Jesus, at God's initiative, is like coming home. Yet as we have found out through these chapters, this is harder than it sounds. Jesus left no hard and fast rules, no guidance on relationship structures or on the best direction in which to go. Whenever anyone asked, he would merely say: 'What do you think? Come and see and make up your own mind'.

This freedom tends to become overwhelmed, these days, by a confused sense of what is of value and what our priorities should be. Everything and everyone has to be efficient and accountable. Results count. In school, league table positions and successful examination results matter. So, too, do balanced budgets and maximum pupil rolls. Drives towards efficiency and good results affect our local police station, social services, surgery and hospital as well as our neighbourhood schools.

Results do matter, Jesus claims, in God's work too. My final watercolour choice illustrates this. The tracks in our first watercolour led to the boats involved in the fishing business. Our tracks should, by invitation, lead us on a new

fishing business, God's business. Jesus chose and put his trust in some very ordinary people to carry on his work after he left earth. They were his friends who had sometimes let him down, sometimes totally misunderstood what he was saying or doing, sometimes even denied knowing him. Yet if he had misplaced that trust in them his ministry would have been for nothing and we would not be contemplating which of God's tracks to follow today. His trust was, however, well placed and we can choose.

I have identified some interesting signposts along our personal walk. It was George Russell who remarked once that there are as many ways of climbing to the stars as there are people to climb. So it is with our Christian pilgrimages. In a way, by walking, we begin a giant jigsaw puzzle, building it up as we go along, analysing each piece until the puzzle, eventually, is complete. Piecing the jigsaw together, though, is only part. Working it out in our lives, piece by piece, determines how far we are determined to travel.

Our walk is an experience for anyone; there are

no barriers and no one is disallowed from walking. What makes teaching, for me, so rewarding is the opportunity to meet such a tremendous variety of people, with different personalities, different problems, aspirations and outlooks on life. I thank God for experiencing this as part of a church community, too. Faith is built and shaped by our local circumstances, by events and the people we meet. But it is also moulded by the way we dream, reaching out beyond the constraints of our local landscape.

Selwyn Hughes, in his book *The Divine Eagle* sees the beginning of our experience of faith like an eagle being pushed out of its nest so as to learn to fly. He is convinced that, mostly, we are content to settle for what we know best, rather than be adventurous; we are content to be comfortable and not take risks. In so doing we often seem satisfied with the little picture and lose the opportunity to be part of a bigger jigsaw. Yet we are all designed to think big thoughts, to dream and enact a creative vision, and there is nothing more exhilarating than to risk something in faith. Sometimes it will fail

and we are back to the start, like our roller-coaster ride. Whatever our experiences, it is God who sets us walking on our tracks again and encourages us to walk that little bit farther.

While walking we will feel, at times, miserable and depressed, insecure and uncertain. We may even feel lost and need to begin again. We will need encouragement and support. But our faith does recreate, renew and invigorate when opportunities allow us, as friends, to do God's business along the way, whatever that may entail. If God is real to us, then we can more meaningfully show this to others and that is something worth hanging on to as we try to keep our tracks in view on the personal beach we each must walk.

'Blessed is the man who perseveres under trial, because when he has stood the test he will receive the crown of life that God has promised to those who love him' (James 1:12). What do you believe the crown of life to be?

How big should we think? What risks should we be prepared to take in faith?

'Peter Smith is a teacher who has dipped into his rich treasure chest of experience and wisdom, brought out some wonderful jewels and polished them until they sparkle for the reader. His Christian reflections on everyday events come from the heart and go to the heart.

I have long admired Graham Clarke's witty style, and his watercolours are another generous collection of jewels. Graham is a wonderfully skilled and assured artist with a light touch and a puckish sense of humour. Text and pictures are perfectly complementary, and together they make up a really delightful book – moving, thoughtful, witty, wise and very attractive.'

The Very Rev. Nicholas Bury, Dean of Gloucester

'In this short book, Peter Smith, a Reader in the diocese of Rochester and a secondary school teacher of many years experience, reflects on his personal understanding of people, places and events. In doing so, he points us to prayer and to God who is in Christ, encouraging us to join with him as he seeks to make sense of the human condition. The result is a book that echoes the everyday with refreshing honesty and openness, and yet goes further, offering glimpses of the eternal. He embraces both sorrow and celebration, with biblical insights informing his reflections. Combined with the work of the artist, Graham Clarke, whose images of the Kentish landscape and of the Christian story have delighted many, Peter Smith's heartfelt words make this book a track to follow with much reward.'

The Rt. Rev. Michael Nazir-Ali, Bishop of Rochester

The author, **Dr Peter Smith**, a geography teacher, is also a deputy headteacher and head of sixth form at Oakwood Park Grammar School, Maidstone. Married with two daughters, he loves walking and travel.

The illustrator, **Graham Clarke**, is one of Britain's most popular and best-selling artists. He specialises in traditional landscapes depicting English rural life. Examples of his work are held by many institutions, including the British Museum, the Library of Congress in Washington, and the Hiroshima Peace Museum.